# notes on the assemblage

# notes on the
# assemblage

juan felipe herrera

City Lights Books | San Francisco

Cover art: collage by Juan Felipe Herrera


Library of Congress Cataloging-in-Publication Data
on file

paper: 978-0-87286-697-3
cloth: 978-0-87286-710-9


City Lights books are published at the City Lights Bookstore
261 Columbus Avenue, San Francisco, CA 94133
www.citylights.com

*For Margarita*

*For Bobby Robles, my brother-in-law, Beto Quintana, my cousin, and poets on the flourishing road —*

*for Michele Serros and Alfsonsito Texidor, RIP*

*When I run, it doesn't mean much —*
*it's a world with a streak across it,*
*and I run up or down or flat along that streak*
*to make the wind sing the way it sings sometimes*
— Marvin Bell, from "When I Run"


*Gracias a la vida que me ha dado tanto*
*Me dio el corazón que agita su marco*

*Thanks to life which has given me all*
*It gave me a heart that beats against its wall*
—Violeta Parra, from "Gracias a la vida"

# Contents

# notes on the
# assemblage

## it can begin with clouds

it can begin with clouds   how they fray   how they enter
then how they envelop the earth
in a second or two they vanish                  you
touch them they take you       you find yourself in their absence
sometimes you read them somehow
          the separation the losses the sky yes
it is the sky they were talking about        the character for sky
you are there now
you have always been there              now
                    where there is fire and
thunder-face behind the torn universe   you can see this
how it shreds itself so you can see this    that
is all there is then
nothing again then you again and              the clouds
come to you     and you pass

# ayotzinapa

From the ferocity of pig driven to holiness . . .
They Lion grow.

*—Phil Levine, from "They Feed They Lion"*

## Ayotzinapa

*para los estudiantes, para México, para el mundo*

Íbamos de Ayotzinapa hacia Iguala para decirle al alcade que
queríamos fondos para nuestra escuela rural para maestros y
maestras era una protesta por nuestra escuela que es solo para
maestros y maestras rurales nada más nada menos protestábamos
solo por obtener algunos fondos fuimos rodeados por la policía
y sus cómplices nos dispararon quemaron nuestros cuerpos nos
desmembraron y en bolsas de basura nos arrojaron al río pero aún
seguimos aún marchamos desde aquí desde las entrañas de México
este río que inunda todos los salones todas las universidades y todos
los pisos de los palacios de los emperadores aún seguimos a los
veinticuatro años de edad nos abrimos paso a través de la masacre
aquí desde donde nacimos desde donde morimos hacia todas las
ciudades del mundo hacia todos los estudiantes y maestras y maestros
del mundo protestando en todas las calles súbitamente quebrando
incandescentes

nadie supo nadie lo vió
       aquí dejamos este número         43 para ti
            porque éramos    43 nosotros

no
somos
desechables

*9-26-14*

—*42 estudiantes de la Escuela Normal de Ayotzinapa desaparecieron después de
que la policía de la ciudad de Iguala, Guerrero, México abrió fuego contra los auto-
buses en que viajaban y secuestró un grupo de 43.*

## Ayotzinapa

*for the students, for Mexico, for the world*

From Ayotzinapa we were headed toward Iguala to say to the
mayor that we wanted funds for our rural school for teachers
it was a protest for our school that is all rural teachers nothing
more nothing less we were protesting for funds that is all we were
surrounded by police and their cronies they fired their guns they
burned us they dismembered us in trash bags they threw us into the
river yet we continue yet we march from here from the bowels of
Mexico this river that floods all the schools and all the universities
and all the floors of the emperors' palaces we continue at twenty-
four years of age we make way through the massacre here from
where we were born and from where we died toward all the cities
in the world toward all the students and teachers in the world
demonstrating on all the streets sprung open
incandescent

no one knew it no one saw it
      we are leaving this number     43 for you
           because there were    43 of us

we are
not disposable


*9-26-14*

—*42 students from the Ayotzinapa Normal School went missing after police in the
city of Iguala, Guerrero, Mexico opened fire on their buses and kidnapped a group
of 43.*

## Y si el hombre con el choke-hold

Y si el hombre con el choke-hold la llave final tumba al hombre parado
por qué vive y si el hombre muerto ya se esfumó por qué se yergue y
por qué se escucha ese clic el sonido que produce el alma cuando se va
aunque nadie lo sepa y si la mujer se queda por qué es ella el
crisol el fuego por qué es ella la voz y si la voz nunca es oída
por qué resuena a través de 9 generaciones y si era un adolescente con
un pavoneo por qué está ahora postrado y si la policía tenía razón y la corte
estuvo de acuerdo y el gobernador habló sumiso ante las masas por qué
están perdidos en el desierto infinito y si los saqueadores cortaron la pared
y partieron el vino por qué están aún abrasados de sed y si protestamos
por qué se quiebra la calle a nuestro paso por qué no nos ofrece *Aquí
tomad mi agua* y si todas las leyes son Libertad para ti para mí por qué no
hablamos y si ese árbol permanece detrás de ti verde con sus últimos
dos brazos en alto hinchados de sangre por qué no sufre

    por
        qué
            florece antorchas

## And if the man with the choke-hold

And if the man with the choke-hold pulls the standing man down
why does he live and if the dead man is gone why does he rise and
why is there a clicking sound the sound the soul makes when it leaves
even though no one knows and if the woman stays why is she the
crucible the fire why is she the voice and if the voice is never heard
why does it resound for 9 generations and if it was a teen with
a swagger why is he still prone and if the police were right and the court
was in agreement and the governor spoke humble facing the masses why
are they lost in the infinite desert and if looters broke the wall and split
the wine why are they still scorched with thirst and if we march
why does the street divide as we pass by why does it not offer us *Here
take my water* and if all the laws are Freedom for you for me why do we
not speak and if that tree stands behind you green with its last two
    limbs up
swollen with blood why does it not suffer

why
      does it
           blossom torches

## Almost Livin' Almost Dyin'
*for all the dead*

& hear my streets
with ragged beats & the beats
are too beat to live so the graves push out with
hands that cannot touch the makers of light & the
sun flames down through the roofs & the roots that slide
to one side & the whistlin' fires of the cops & the cops
in the shops do what they gotta do & your body's
on the fence & your ID's in the air & the shots
get fired & the gas in the face & the tanks
on your blood & the innocence all around & the
spillin' & the grillin' & the grinnin' & the game of Race
no one wanted & the same every day so U fire &
eat the smoke thru your long bones & the short mace
& the day? This last sweet Swisher day that turns to love
& no one knows how it came or what it is or what it says
or what it was or what for or from what gate
is it open is it locked can U pull it back to your life
filled with bitter juice & demon angel eyes even though
you pray & pray mama says you gotta sing she says
you got wings but from what skies from where could
they rise what are the things the no-things called love
how can its power be fixed or grasped so the beats
keep on blowin' keep on flyin' & the moon tracks your bed
where you are alone or maybe dead & the truth
carves you carves you & calls you back still alive
cry cry the candles by the last four trees still soaked
in Michael Brown red and Officer Liu red and
Officer Ramos red and Eric Garner whose
last words were not words they were just breath

askin' for breath they were just burnin' like me like
we are all still burnin' can you hear me
can you feel me swaggin' tall & driving low &
talkin' fine & hollerin' from my corner crime & fryin'
                                        against the wall

almost livin' almost dyin'
almost livin' almost dyin'

the view with
no one

## You & I Belong in this Kitchen

longtime hermano Bob        tells me
one of the monks in brown directs us to the deep sink
made of two sinks the hose & the silver table where all
the spoons & metal tongs are clean
wait at the entrance for directions the monk gave me
but he is in there & points me to another sink
made of two sinks & a silver table where all
the spoons & metal tongs are clean
scrub off the rice burned at the bottom
clinging to the sides of the steel
outside working the hole in the earth
three monks in brown stir the blackish pots boiling
four kettles of mud cakes for the new lunar year
the dragon the people the monastery the mountains
one monk stands staring into the nothing
no thoughts around him
the other monk descends through the colorless fog two
children angle an exploded tree limb back & forth
so the sparks play with them      to the left
the meditation hall is curved & faces Escondido
down below where my father drove his army truck
& pulled our trailer to a stop on Lincoln Road in '54
I watered spidered corn & noticed the deportations
little friends gone the land left to freeze alone
lunch is served we go to the line the spoons
& the speckled tongs await by the brown rice
white rice eggplant kimchi & a grey pot
pour the seaweed soup we go with our tray & sit
the mud cakes are ribboned in red & gold & green
there is a way to do this

it requires listening & seeing &
silence          silence the bell rings
longtime hermano Bob & I      at the parking lot
we leave brown cloth                    brown cloth
naked spoons      naked pots
steam          rises from the sink &      the view
the view with no one

## Here and There

I sit and meditate — my dog licks her paws
on the red-brown sofa
so many things somehow
it all is reduced to numbers letters figures
without faces or names only jagged lines
across the miles half-shadows
going into shadow-shadow then destruction          the infinite light

here and there               cannot be overcome
it is the first drop of ink

## Ourselves

atop the mountain rain into
snow wind glass          enter collide

new lives up down  sideways ascensions
below  we are dry          abandoned
without the loved ones dissolved
weeping we stand

they crash at the heights   the mist edge
ripped from          our longings
sudden                          harmonies  become
vastness  wild              dark streaked
the light severe                concertos
at the peak                      whirl

whirl   for a moment then back again

into themselves        ourselves

## White Dove — Found Outside Don Teriyaki's

On
Cedar & Herndon going nowhere brought her home
bought her seeds a rabbit cage & carried her out
everyday & let her fly in the room next to my bedroom
I was concerned about her — I asked myself
what can I do
she is not happy she is not free she dances when
I take the cage outside & set it on the angular table
in the breezeway then the sun waves through
and the trees sway before noon when the sister doves
Blue Jays call & peck at the seeds she spills
she steps to one side to the other and back
and forth she peers at me through the wires
I take her inside
she purrs she calls — if I release her she is going to
stumble then Jack Hawk will shred her so
I'll keep her in the cage — I tell myself

## Notes on the Assemblage

use black & gray & speckled white construction paper
use stripped scraped & perforated construction paper
use found paper
use cardboard / wet &
mashed
overlay on old encyclopedias / sheets with images
something like Kentridge or Delmore Schwartz
use soap to brush them
draw with pencil & marker
draw the soap & noodles some stones
draw with pencil and marker for outline
11 x 14 sheet
draw the muddy camp the bus the pier
the toilet line
close-ups too
—how we look
at each other
what we have on our faces
                    you can cross thought through it
you can escape into it and out
through its holes its gases
our faces
have changed
can we go back
you can't wash it off
but you can erase it

## On the Verge of Drowning

into these open sheet glass waters      go down
the last faces     the rose solar skinned mouths
say something — it is
not too late (but words do not count here)     you
must dive in   keep   your
bruise inked arm here     naked
half-broken body in star-shape   reddish
violet waves   plasmas
a teacher & her emerging     coffee cup
a student & his wild clock scroll
a woman with a basket ornate fibers an eye
against     quantum forces   against

sirens levers marching charcoal   stained
armies with handsome cages     for heads
break away you must break away i mean
i
must
break away     clasp
   falling hands     the
     disappearing

here     take this
woman black jeweled basket

## You Throw a Stone

           you throw a stone
i throw               a stone
i                           throw a stone
you                              throw a stone
then a rocket
a rocket                       comes down
here                         i lay
                 next to you
we are
brothers in a way                  w/o a sky
my father's house        is empty        your
mother's house has        no amber light
      as it once had   even the sun
cannot penetrate
the open field where        you and i
once played    (in our separate dreams)
burns &                burns
      those stones   what were they
        where did they come from

hard hooks

## Los Angeles Barrio Sonnet for Wanda Coleman
*Word-Caster of Live Coals of Love, RIP*

Wanda Coleman word-caster of live coals of Watts & LA you hear
LA yes all the barrios & raise up the voice of the young & the
bards inside all hearts blastin' & keepin' life alive in alleys become
precious & courts where the jesters drill the King's coral brooch
it was Wanda who set the moat on fire you yes pillaged bright
& dug the core the word the sonnet in Coltrane fix what was
this American thing of Race against Race you said what was this
under-realm where we tango in desire & headless hate & unborn
& the fire wheels inside the blood the bliss where? You in the
multi-night

in song silvered
in street rally quiver
a blues beyond so you prism now
under desert moon alone below & above
dressed in saguaro & cholla & spike
we congregate &
we dance uncanny no mumble        we bow
place our hands open     face    you    now
Wanda Coleman word-caster of live          coals of love

in gratitude
     we stand & rise

*(11-23-2013)*

## Hard Hooks that Fold You Down to Your Knees
*for Jack Gilbert, RIP*

In Soho, NYC — at Dunkin' Donuts of all places, a year ago —
hanging out with Gerald Stern so we talked like always. About
everything, about Paris in the '50s. The conversation was good,
you know about selling black market typewriters and other goods.
We came to a stop, Jerry slowed and spoke of Jack. The words are
jumbled up now if I could recall them maybe about Jack being in a
Berkeley home with Alzheimer's having saved serious money just to
hand it over to caretakers. It wasn't the words. It was the tenderness
in Stern's voice. That's all you need sometimes to say a lot about a
good man — a poet with all the power Jack was known for — the
hard-hooks that fold you down to your knees. Back in SF when I
was starting out and you were getting your second wind.


*(11-14-2012)*

## Bisbee Poetry Festival, Southern Arizona, 1985

*for Jayne Cortez, RIP*

It was you &
Rochelle Owens & her many words for one word
& Ashbery who spoke of Nordic myth & the mystic house
Yes lightning hit when he said that
& Acker who wrote Don Quixote we must steal it she said
Ed Sanders played his piano tie wired
his own harmonics near the Beat heart I shimmied on stage
my Dallas Cowboys jersey & my Viet Nam jungle boots
we were
about to turn into this fire-world without measure
you saw that you burned with that
you saw that

*(1-5-2013)*

## Hey Phil

*for Phil Levine, RIP*

They are writing about you Phil — you know
good stuff — the prizes   Detroit and that
poem where you said in past lives you
were a wild sun-crested fox being chased
by "ladies and gentlemen on horseback" —
you said you would wake up with the poem
ready that it slipped untangled from a dream
all you had to do was sit up and write
the stage was a poem too — even though
most of us were too prepared you
preferred to joke before we went on
before the poetry light hit us on the face
it did not matter to you — you just carved
chiseled punctured rotated jitterbugged
and whirred past a distant gate


*(2-14-2015)*

## Oda para José Montoya
*(9-25-2013), QDEP*

oye y ahora cómo le vamos hacer
con tu pachuko portfolio y ese tripe de los
tirilongos del Segundo y los campesinos con
paliacates en Revolución y esa tórika
de las tres calles — trenzadas en una
                          Frontera Blvd. — y
ahora ya sales en ese Bomber VW Van Nirvana
pintado mural solar blast-off incense copal danzante
la bendición de Tonantzín y esta tierrita colorada
color chile de Hatch rostizado 20 kilos en saco de ixtle
y ahora tu pintura en llamas en frentes adolescentes
en corazones de generaciones qué más José
tu bondad tu voz de dooby-dooby-doo-wop
píntame los tramos color cielo desarraigado
píntame los drapes color fuego y tutti-frutti
píntame la cara color león del barrio y
color bandera César Chávez Dolores Huerta
y no se te olvide este grito
lo oyes
desde La Logan hasta Sacra — jazz de los '40s
a través del 5 y el 99 — ¡Que Viva José Montoya!
para siempre siemprecito    carnal


c/s

## Ode for José Montoya
*(9-25-2013), RIP*

So how are we gonna do it now
with your Pachuko Portfolio & that trip about
the Tirilongo bad dudes from Second Ward & the campesinos with
hard work headbands in Revolution & that rap
of the three streets — braided
                              Border Frontera Blvd. — &
now you come out on the Bomber VW Van Nirvana
painted mural solar blast-off incense copal danzante sacred
the blessing of Tonantzín & the tiny earth red
color of chile from Hatch roasted 20 kilos in ixtle gunnysack
& now your art fire on adolescent foreheads
in the hearts of generations José
your kindness your voice dooby-dooby-doo-wop
paint me the flying coat color of flame & tutti-frutti
paint me the face color lion barrio &
color of César Chávez Dolores Huerta flag
& do not forget the howl
you hear it
all the way from Logan Heights Barrio to Sacra — jazz of the '40s
across I-5 & 99 ¡Viva José Montoya!
forever a sweet forever    my brother

c/s

lucid and
undecipherable
tasks

## Lucid and Undecipherable Tasks

& i leaned
against the rock it was the storm
i lay there opened

upon the stones and ferns against the leaves that spoke
and held my flesh the trees
the red-shouldered hawk it was the eagle
it caressed my face held it up to the lightning beaks of night
the infinite the eye the void
lucid and undecipherable tasks all things

become one it was my breath upon you
breath alone and full free and still
revealed by the moon and the moon the wild sickle swan and
i ascended
through the fire

## The Soldier in the Empty Room

*after Rigoberto Gonzalez's "Soldier in Mictlán"*

> It's not necessary to say anything.
> The paper counts out the dead —
> Twenty million.
>
> — *Judita Vaiciunaite, from "Twenty Million"*
> *(Translated by Jonas Zdanys)*

Near the bed made of leaves and torn handkerchiefs
windows of rags tobacco smoke there were
women scouring the ground
as if the soldier's bones could curl and speak and sing:

*"Oh, the hills are merry,*
*our green trees are filled with song*
*our baked round loaves we carry,*
*now, all our woes are gone."*

The last soldier dreamt awake
in the empty room of the empty town.
He said: "I saw the sky in pieces
I saw the stars that fell too soon."

"We are here to fill your crimson mouth,
from the north to the south," the stars said.
"We are knocking at your humble winter door."

"Come," the forest nymph said to the last soldier,
"I'll take your guns with so many names."

"This is Miroslava," the soldier said,
　　　　"who caressed my face of holes and moths."

"This is Marina,
          who gave me a wooden cup of blackish moon."
"This is Furia,
          who never listened,
          who turned his back, a brother I once had."
"This is Lucha,
          who blessed me even though I never returned,
          who was tiny and sacred, forgiving and tiny again,
          — the one who cut me into life."
"This is Peiter,
          who galloped ahead,
          on a handsome silver horse. He was painted with thunder
          in a country of soot and long-arm children who
          dragged themselves without a mother of milk
          or straw or silky wires
          or a father
          of ovens, tables or crows or desires."

"Pieter, take me," the soldier said in the empty room
but Pieter dissolved with tall fire sweeping him,
scarves of fire from his crooked neck and
fire on his wide forehead.

"Come," the soldier said and pulled
toward the window. There were tiny skies
made of rock and shells and songs made of splinters
and water and spit — "The clouds," Pieter said,

"for the flesh that I once
cast onto the enemies drooling
and kicking and guffawing and burning."
The last soldier stood up in the empty room and noticed
the forest nymph who revealed his hair of sun-broken rivers

of men and cannon shells spent and
dogs with satchels.

The soldier sat on the gray table,
touched bread turned to stone,
from afar he heard the hungry
marching through hives and the bells
of their helmets against the black
jeweled trees and — the shoes

so many shoes shrapnel-bitten
pounding, shuffling by themselves,
tearing all around then stopping to
wait — for him.

i do not
know what
a painting
does

## Jackrabbits, Green Onions & Witches Stew

Jackrabbits, green onions & witches stew
3 dollars & upside down lemons & you
Dinky planet on a skateboard of dynamite
O, what to do, chile peppers, Mrs. Oops
Dr. What, Mr. Space Station unscrewed
The *Redbook of Ants* says you better run
No sireee, LOL, blowin' my bubble gum sun

## Tasmano

*after Alfredo Arreguín's paintings*

Tasmano
                    tasmano
                              let me
                                        hold you
                                                  & let me
                                        bury myself
                              into your seasonalsalmon skin
                    ice disappearance
                                        blackness lips
cabellera máscaras cholula culebra gold spattered spiral breasts la
    lumbre Michoacana
de las cumbres brujas ripping spirit flesh blue madness locuras dentro
greener yellowness tehuana tehuanasalt storms arms i bow to
your tejido king kodiak spirit in your sacred belly egg
man woman flayed scales fins gone lives
gone face destroyed turquoise
azar albedrío thrown &
unknown

## En la media medianoche

Rumba y chocolate en la media medianoche
y la noche rabanera bajo la tierra que está ciega
abrázame en la mesa rezandera y el platillo de hormiguera
vamos a Carrara a cantarle al conde de azufres y de cifras y arrecifes
      pero nada lloviznando por el paredón
          por el paredón y carruajes de hueseras
            lloviznando lloviznando
así ando.

## In the mid of midnight

Rumba and chocolate in the mid of midnight
and the turniping night under the earth that has gone blind
embrace me on the table of the prayer-woman and the anthill dish
let us go to Carrara to sing to the Count of Sulfurs and ciphers and reefs
      but nothing raining by the killing wall
           by the killing wall and carriages of the skeleton carrier
               raining light rain
like this I walk.

# Fulgencio salió de Oaxaca hacia El Norte

*a partir del arte de Fulgencio Lazo, Seattle, WA, 2014*

Los ojos verdes el mármol de vida y muerte el ajedrez
y al azar los tejidos de gis de municipio de arpa fugaz
donde caminamos un lienzo entre blanco y anaranjado
el albedrío de pueblos y más que nada el guinda loco
de caderas y brazos rasgados pero no te das cuenta

        los amantes los azulejos secretos
            un copal renace un rehilete de madres
                        hirviendo la tierra

y otras desarraigando las cimas de orquestas y carnes
secas nuestras risas el amor de coco de piña de
ciruela de penitencia de mil generaciones y migraciones
piel de calabaza hacia Norte al Sur al Norte y oyes
los violines de perros que te olfatean a los que no

        les regalaste chicharrón o son
            garabatos estrellas tartamudas

                    o son

papalotes clavados de costillas y lenguas serpientes o brujas
o un niño que despertó al mundo con aceites zapotecos
planeta negro ferrocarril encendido traje de cruces y
almas de lagartos más almas más tejidos geométricos
más abejas picando eléctricas flautas tuyas mías letritas
noches máscaras amarillas iglesias blancas y un tigre paseándose
        en medio de todo
           juegos de luz tambores y maíz
               más vuelos más aguas para el Gozón

     así así vamos
        por allí va por aquí viene

# Fulgencio left Oaxaca toward El Norte

*after the art of Fulgencio Lazo, Seattle, WA, 2014*

The eyes green marble stone of life & death the Chess
& the gamble the weavings of chalk of município of fury harp
where we walk a canvas a bit between white & orange
the will of pueblos & more than anything the crazy reddish blue
of hips & arms clawed but you do not see it

      the lovers & arms the secret puffed bluish tiles
         a honeyed incense opens up a wand of mothers
                        boiling the earth

& others uprooting the peaks of orchestras & meats
sun-dried our smiles of love of coconut & pineapple
dry plum penitence of a thousand generations & migrations of
calabaza skin toward Norte toward Sur to Norte & you hear
the dog violins that sniff-sniff you & those that you did not

           offer chicharrón or are they
             gibberish scrawl mute stars
                   or are they

kites rib-nailed & serpent tongues or witches
or a child that woke the earth with Zapotec oils
black planet locomotive on fire a suit of crosses &
lizard souls more souls geometrically woven
more honeybees prickling electric flutes yours mine tiny letters
night masks yellow ones churches white ones & a tiger pacing
      in the middle of everything
         games of light & drums & maíz
            more flights more waters for El Gozón

        like that like that we go
          through there it goes over here he goes

## i do not know what a painting does

i do not know what a painting does it
lean against the wall — it could be any color of wall or house
in the kitchen on the refrigerator or next to the hard-carved
wooden masks the mirror that wakens when you pass by
you add grease you tap it with the palette knife the paste
moves then it thins its metals into the glazes a kind
of staccato it could be a self-portrait with all the difficulties
veiled in the half-dark jacket slapped with burning rectangles
titanium white as if they were confetti all in stillness
what else could it be it is flat it is smaller than you
even if it is a wall or a fence or a sky where you move
your brushes — what does it do that is my question
it looks back I think that is why you paint you are
waiting for the thing-in-itself to come back to you to
greet you in its odd oblong stunted manner its elegance
it feeds you it surrounds you wherever you go you
do not have to walk into it your tiny room it merely
poses for you when you are at your beginnings then
it follows you passes you dissolves ahead of you where
it is waiting for you when you get there you will not
know it until you see that it is seeing you seeing you

## Radiante (s)

*after Olga Albizu's painting "Radiante," 1967*

Jestered ochre yellow my umber Rothko
divisions my Brooklyns with Jerry Stern
black then oranged gold leaf & tiny skulls
perforations Dada sugar bread of Oaxacan
ecstasy Lorca's green horse the daffodil head
corruptions of the State in tenor exhalation
saxophonics blossomings rouged monkey
Dalí roll down the keys the high G's
underStreets of the undeRealms my hair.

Throttle up into hyper-city correlations =
compassion compassion

                    the void extends

borderbus

## Tomorrow I Leave to El Paso

see my brother-in-law with a styled shirt
in spite of his cancer below
then a small dinner in the evening the next day
no one knows except I may be on the road
Mesquite where my father settled in '31
forty-five minutes west then a left you go in
sister Sarita waits for me on Abby Street
after decades in separate families we just met
now I hear the clock snap I swipe an ant
time to walk my dogs five blocks and back
a different route to soothe the mind
it is the same one but I am hopeful

## Borderbus

A dónde vamos  where are we going
Speak in English or the guard is going to come
A dónde vamos  where are we going
Speak in English or the guard is gonna get us hermana
Pero qué hicimos  but what did we do
Speak in English come on
Nomás sé unas pocas palabras  I just know a few words

You better figure it out hermana the guard is right there
See the bus driver

Tantos días y ni sabíamos para donde íbamos
So many days and we didn't even know where we were headed

I know where we're going
Where we always go
To some detention center to some fingerprinting hall or cube
Some warehouse warehouse after warehouse

Pero ya nos investigaron ya cruzamos ya nos cacharon
Los federales del bordo qué más quieren
But they already questioned us we already crossed over they
already grabbed us the Border Patrol what more do they want

We are on the bus now
that is all

A dónde vamos te digo salí desde Honduras
No hemos comido nada y dónde vamos a dormir

Where are we going I am telling you I came from Honduras
We haven't eaten anything and where are we going to sleep

I don't want to talk about it just tell them
That you came from nowhere
I came from nowhere
And we crossed the border from nowhere
And now you and me and everybody else here is
On a bus to nowhere you got it?

Pero por eso nos venimos para salir de la nada
But that's why we came to leave all that nothing behind

When the bus stops there will be more nothing
We're here hermana

Y esas gentes quiénes son
no quieren que siga el camión
No quieren que sigamos
Están bloqueando el bus
A dónde vamos ahora
Those people there who are they
they don't want the bus to keep going
they don't want us to keep going
now they are blocking the bus
so where do we go

What?

He tardado 47 días para llegar acá no fue fácil hermana
45 días desde Honduras con los coyotes los que se — bueno
ya sabes lo que les hicieron a las chicas allí mero en frente
de nosotros pero qué íbamos a hacer y los trenes los trenes

cómo diré hermana cientos de
nosotros como gallinas como topos en jaulas y verduras
pudriendóse en los trenes de miles me oyes de miles y se resbalaban
de los techos y los desiertos de Arizona de Tejas sed y hambre
sed y hambre dos cosas sed y hambre día tras día hermana
y ahora aquí en este camión y quién sabe a dónde
vamos hermana fíjate vengo desde Brownsville dónde nos amarraron
y ahora en California pero todavía no entramos y todavía el bordo
está por delante
It took me 47 days to get here it wasn't easy hermana
45 days from Honduras with the coyotes the ones that — well
you know what they did to las chicas
right there in front of us so what were we supposed
to do and the trains the trains how can I tell you hermana hundreds
of us like chickens like gophers in cages and vegetables
rotting on trains of thousands you hear me of thousands and they slid
from the rooftops and the deserts of Arizona and Texas thirst and hunger
thirst and hunger two things thirst and hunger day after day hermana
and now here on this bus of who-knows-where we are going
hermana listen I come from Brownsville where they tied us up
and now in California but still we're not inside and still the border
lies ahead of us

I told you to speak in English even un poquito
the guard is going to think we are doing something
people are screaming outside
they want to push the bus back

Pero para dónde le damos hermana
por eso me vine
le quebraron las piernas a mi padre
las pandillas mataron a mi hijo
solo quiero que estemos juntos

tantos años hermana
separados
But where do we go hermana
that's why I came here
they broke my father's legs
gangs killed my son
I just want us to be together
so many years hermana
pulled apart

What?

Mi madre me dijo que lo más importante
es la libertad la bondad y la buenas acciones
con el prójimo
My mother told me that the most important thing
is freedom kindness and doing good
for others

What are you talking about?
I told you to be quiet

La libertad viene desde muy adentro
allí reside todo el dolor de todo el mundo
el momento en que purguemos ese dolor de nuestras entrañas
seremos libres y en ese momento tenemos que
llenarnos de todo el dolor de todos los seres
para liberarlos a ellos mismos
Freedom comes from deep inside
all the pain of the world lives there
the second we cleanse that pain from our guts
we shall be free and in that moment we have to
fill ourselves up with all the pain of all beings

to free them — all of them

The guard is coming well
now what        maybe they'll take us
to another detention center we'll eat we'll have a floor
a blanket toilets water and each other
for a while

No somos nada y venimos de la nada
pero esa nada lo es todo si la nutres de amor
por eso venceremos
We are nothing and we come from nothing
but that nothing is everything, if you feed it with love
that is why we will triumph

We are everything hermana
Because we come from everything

## The Soap Factory

**Martínez:**
Soap soap soap soap
all we do is make soap here
soap on the belt
in & out it comes in & out   forever
it goes & nobody knows who makes it
you got that Schwartz? Nobody
you know I know all the guys here know &
sergeant García knows right sarge?

**Schwartz:**
Don't mess with him this may not be his best day
swinging that baton all dressed up for nothing
but us guys on the line me and you and Lim
hey Lim yeah get with it you getting that soap out?
you better get it right — soap for the
bourgeoisie right Martínez?

**Martínez:**
What does the bourgeoisie need it for
they don't use soap Schwartz you know that

**Schwartz:**
What?  Read my lips —
authority confidence persuasion secrets and guilt
every aspect of power is in that
piece of crap soap

**Martínez:**

You ever seen soap this big
it's as thick as one of those Caribbean ocean liners

**Schwartz:**

But it is made by you — and me
and each and everyone of us
that's why we are locked up in this dingy
Alcatraz of manure on this candy ass line-up
dressed up in these silly putty gowns
in these funky plaid overalls and dunce clown hats
these McDonald's leftover caps and these
loose Cowboys' loser football jerseys
year after year with a sentence
on our heads got that? A sentence . . .
so shuddup and get with it
it's almost lunch time & I want
to get back to my house &
listen to my show a little Jeopardy
never hurt anybody

**Martínez:**

I mean I never seen soap this big
like back in Atizapán de Zaragoza
we used to wash our pantalones out
in the yard next to the pigs
in this cement block sink
with this phlegm-colored soap
people here don't even use this
so why on earth are we making it
can you answer that Mr. Birdbrain

**Schwartz:**

The soap is not for the big guys
it's for the little guys right right
I said the bourgeoisie Martínez
they sell it to us they sell it to us
get with it here comes you know who

**García:**

You crybabies got a problem?
or do you want me to write you up
and hand you a problemo?
That's what I thought
just a bunch of crybabies
move your hands fast Martínez
that's better — and
you Schwartz I am telling you
if you even lift
your hands one inch above your waist
you are mine got that

**Schwartz:**

That's it:
I am outta here Martínez
no more soap
no more soap
no more dreaming in soap
no more soap up your nostrils
no more soap in between your cheeks
no more soap that's it
no more washing
no more cleaning
no more polishing

no more see-through phlegm that isn't skin or bone or wax
no more soap            that's it

**Martínez:**
I am going back to the cafeteria
at least you can eat the little lemon pies
that come back half-eaten from the trays
and the cranberry juice
and those hamburger buns with sesame seeds

let's ask Sarge for some ducats
give us a pass
you and I been here for at least fifteen years
right Schwartz?
we deserve a little better

**Schwartz:**
He's read your report Martínez
he's got that little report on you

**Martínez:**
Ah come on
who's gonna read that stuff
so I did a little thing to someone
last year it's over allright?

**Schwartz:**
The cafeteria cakes and little drinks
of red-colored water
is that it Martínez
I thought your people were all about
Revolution and Justice so

what happened to that Martínez
what happened to Revolution and Justice?

**Martínez:**
My people?
What people? I am here
alone Schwartz look around
can you see me or are your glasses
cracked?

You are my people Schwartz
you and Lim

**Schwartz:**
When my father was beaten
I just lay there pretending I was dead
I was a kid you hear that Martínez
just a kid what could I do
against those men all put together
like they were the answer to the world
in that mud world where my papa and I lived
in that muddy wired fenced-in bubble of crap

this soap
they want us to dish it out to the little people to
wash it all away just like that
they want you to walk around bristling in lilac
or lavender or some kind of flowery grease
but as long as I am here
it's not gonna happen Martínez I spit
into every slab of mud soap that
comes my way

**Martínez:**

What are you talking about Schwartz?

**Schwartz:**

Here let me clean your eyes come on
let's do it let me clean those prickly eyes
those mousy ears the color of wheat and spinach

**Martínez:**

Lim what are you doing?
You are not supposed to leave your station
listen to me
Hey!
Wait!

**Schwartz:**

Bring back that soap!
Hey come on Lim you are going to get us all in trouble
listen hey get
back here Lim!

**Martínez**

What's he doing Schwartz?

**Schwartz:**

Don't ask me

**Martínez**

I think he lost his marbles

**Schwartz:**

Looks like he's scrubbing the wall

**Martínez:**

No one scrubs the wall no one has ever gotten that far
he's popped a hole Schwartz
he's popped a hole through the wall Schwartz
he's stepping out

**Schwartz:**

It doesn't work like that Martinez
this isn't one of those comedies where you wipe your nose
in the middle of everything and think everything is the same
after you're done

**Martínez:**

He's gone Schwartz
he's out there now

**Schwartz:**

He's melting
into the crowd
somewhere
      blood  121       flesh875
Sound iiii

Silencexx
Puls2e

Motioswn and forc1292e3cecdwcwdoi

                                    u

## but i was the one that saw it (drone aftermath)

                                        Ak what
ak
lmo
no
no
no
no
LMNO
Lmno
Llmno
Lmnoooooooo
          Mn
          Mn
          Wn   oooooo


          I   CA


                                              e

                                              E

          EA

                                              Ee



     Rrrrrrrrrrrrrrrrrrrrrrr r r r rrrrrr rrrrrrrr r r r r rR

rrrrrrrrrrrrrrrrr

                                                        E

        S       n                           E

        I                       C           N   T


        S       P
AK

--

0

S

0

P

0

00000000000000

0
0
0
0
0

0
0
0
0

0000
0
0

000
0
0

0 0 0 0 0 0 0 0 0 0 0

#14928:01

I didn't know why I was dying / From outta nowhere you know /
It happened like that / I saw it all come down / I just kinda kept
on talking and talking / Then I wasn't talking but I was just still /
Standing there with my boots in a ditch


#930288_9

I had this irrational detachment / From everything / That was
going on / People were getting killed / The missiles were coming
down / We were calling the others / But they couldn't hear us or
something / We were back there

There

#1265:

There were some people protesting / They were making a ruckus / I
think they had some kind of agenda and wanted us to join them but /
We were just trying to figure out / What was going on and /


0 0 0

0000
0    0

#17
That's it

I was / holding a baby /we wanted to get married / I was point-
ing at it / I saw it / Everyone else was down / Some were standing
but / but I was the one that saw it

## Numbers, Patterns, Movements & Being

we      are not what we thought — it is
not who we were or
what we want to be
it has nothing to do with being or becoming
or even non-being, which is
what we
always wanted, really

it is merely movement, yes, but —
how we move
from *afar*, we missed this somewhere

we thought about ourselves up close even
though we were not that intimate all along
it has to do — with imperceptible distance

so much so that all that can be perceived
is movement           for example

1, 2  or 8
        anglessudden          quirks

dimensions spatialthings as if
mono-cells in an aqueous      gelled platter
of revolution, of course, that is why
distance is necessary — revolution is
always a potential, that is
a pattern, yes
a specific pattern that can erupt

at
any
given
moment — which requires an observer

not you not me, of course, that's
the old game of identity — the game of
the observed, not the see-r

you see

we are not what we thought — it is
not who we were or
what we want to be

it has nothing to do with being or becoming
or even    non-being, which is what we
always wanted, really

[untitled, unfettered___

        really truly breathe
                unfettered
by the obligatory
frames we cast for ourselves

  it does not matter
nevertheless

the question is
what are you going to do
             with all this life   for
some odd reason
it is yours         you
can live it    not

            all of it   but
you can live it
     for a little
         while  &

if you do
      you really
          will not need
to live all of it

## i am Kenji Goto

*for Kenji Goto & Haruwa Yukawa, for their words,*
*murdered in Syria, January 2015*

even though i am not here
here i am in southern Turkey — i
am heading to Syria. 200,000 killed
— three million refugees. i can go on
with numbers pointed at you
Syria i say
gone your children — torn lost
it is their suffering in all directions
that concerned me yesterday. i am still in Syria
faces of the tiny ones — everywhere
they turn to my notes
these are your words i tell them
my words
are your words i tell them
i am Kenji Goto the man who journeys
in danger  — arid lands orange cloth
kneeling. here in front of you still
mourning for you —

                each one
mourning for Haruwa Yukawa
the poet in front of you
is not the one who walked
to Raqqa — it does not matter
something lives on

       i write  in danger
for lives in danger i — i
am Kenji Goto

## song out here

if i could sing
i'd say everything   you know
from here on the street can you turn around
just for once i am                 here
right behind you
what is that flag what is it made of
maybe it's too late i have
too many questions where did it all come from
what colors is it all made of everything
everything here in the subways
there are so many things and voices
we are going somewhere but i just don't know
somewhere
but i just don't know
          somewhere
do you know where that is i want to sing
so you can hear me and maybe you can tell me
where to go so you can hear me and just maybe
you can tell me where to go
all those hands and legs and faces going places
if i could sing
you would hear me and i would tell you
it's gonna be alright
it's gonna be alright
it's gonna be alright it would be something like that
can you turn around so i can look into your eyes
just for once your eyes
maybe like hers can you see her
and his can you see them i want you to see them
all of us we could be together

if i could sing we would go there
we would run there together
we would live there for a while in that tilted
tiny house by the ocean rising up inside of us
i am on the curb next to a curled up cat
smoking i know it's bad for you but
you know how it is just for once can you turn around
a straight line falling behind you it's me i want to sing
invincible                              bleeding out with love

just for you

we are
remarkably
loud not
masked

## Thich Nhat Hanh I Step With You

step    breathe
step                    breathe


                        — peace flickers at the end of the flame
you sit you speak one word yet the word is impossible

rice brown and eggplant soup green violet
your mind still          for peace
decade upon decade bowing speaking lifting the dead
from your shoulders our hands
this is how you walk — one step we walk with you
one step there
a breath as        you go  as we go

## We Are Remarkably Loud Not Masked

young Jesse Washington —
                    even though you    on the wooden stick
cross of fire bitten charred cut & burned    5 minute jury
April 15, 1916 Waco, Texas shackled & dragged  — lynched
                    you live on


                              Trayvon Martin face down
red juice on the lawn clutching candy rushing home
the hoodie the hoodie the prowler shooter said
upside down shredded night


                                        because of you  you


we march touch hands lean back leap forth
against the melancholy face of tanks & militia    we move
                              walk become
we become        somehow


Eric Garner we scribble your name sip your breath    now
          our breath cannot be choked off our
skin cannot be flamed      totality
                    cannot be cut off
each wrist
each bone
cannot be chained to the abyss
          gnashing levers & polished
                    killer sheets of steel


we are remarkably loud not masked
          rough river colors that cannot be threaded back

hear us
Freddie Gray here                                    with us


                              Jesse Washington Trayvon Martin
Michael Brown the Black Body holy
    Eric Garner  all breath Holy
we weep & sing
as we write
                      as we mobilize & march
                          under the jubilant solar face

## Half-Mexican

Odd to be a half-Mexican, let me put it this way
I am Mexican + Mexican, then there's the question of the half
To say Mexican without the half, well it means another thing
One could say *only Mexican*
Then think of pyramids — obsidian flaw, flame etchings, goddesses with
Flayed visages claw feet & skulls as belts — these are not Mexican
They are existences, that is to say
Slavery, sinew, hearts shredded sacrifices for the continuum
Quarks & galaxies, the cosmic milk that flows into trees
Then darkness
                              What is the other — yes
It is Mexican too, yet it is formless, it is speckled with particles
European pieces? To say colony or power is incorrect
Better to think of Kant in his tiny room
Shuffling in his black socks seeking out the notion of time
Or Einstein re-working the erroneous equation
Concerning the way light bends — all this has to do with
The half, the half-thing when you are a half-being

Time
                Light

How they stalk you & how you beseech them
All this becomes your lifelong project, that is
You are Mexican. One half Mexican the other half
Mexican, then the half against itself.

## Smiling Dragon

from her tin-leaf cave
emptiness through the fire-embroidered mist
this vortex that connects all things   the task
touches earth and no thing the battle
                        at the peak timelessness
seven mountains Taishan

she-dragon smiles & casts her wings

upon the rubble oceans              emperors
kings dynasties all the fascinations of men
columns of smoke   seed & steel

the dragon smiles & round & round
inside her bones the mother-song continues
this vortex that connects all things   the task
touches earth and no thing the battle

## Saturday Nite at the Buddhist Cinema

                                    There were elephants
in cabaret dress reddish & cadmium blue
& dolphins in undetermined incarnations (I felt as if
I had interrupted the process I mean
the organ player had not risen
remember the Castro theatre off of Market?
It was Visconti's *Rocco & His Brothers* & the lights went out maybe
1992 during the Rodney King revolt
the dolphin was working this out somehow tweeting
blinking his tiny saucy eyes I was in the third row as usual
in the middle) there was a horse torn unbridled
immense & stoic being pinned
with a hideous medal by the War Provosts it turned to us &
waited   waited           for someone to take her home
the cow was there

        in a Mexican Pancho Villa outfit
                    spraying everyone with snowflakes &
        you you           should have seen us

how we had realized the Way
how we rubbed the blood off of our faces after the killings &
how we stuck it to the assassins huddled in a shabby corner
you should have seen the Pig Act
the pig           a real pig with a wig in flames
in pinkish pajamas & a cigar doing a Fatty Arbuckle shtick
he even ordered 18 eggs over easy with 18 sides of sourdough
cranberry sauce sardines & a side of pastrami he was
hanging off the window ledge top story of the St. Francis
yodeling to a Gloria Swanson look-alike in a cashmere robe
(it was hilarious it was

what we all dreamed of yes that was it     it
was what we all dreamed of) the chicken in kimono pirouetted
with piquant harpsichord arpeggios
*Sonata in E Major* by Domenico Scarlatti the evil iris
on the side of the cheeky make-up popped
that is when I fell out
slid to the toilet but there were no towels or stalls or water
it was some kind of trick I said & blew my nose
into my sleeve an Italian piece from Beverly Hills 1966
(why was I there
all of a sudden?)


        For the Short Feature everyone shouted
*Where's the Tuna?*
             *We want the Tuna?*
          *We want the Tuna!*
*What about the Tuna?*


The organ rose from the stage
the song *Avremi der Marvikher* jittered the chandeliers
sung by a scrubby lanky tenor in a shredded vest
I had the same Chrysanthemum eyes of exile
I had the same wet braided locks & the black spot
       we all danced with straw-stuffed violas we lost ourselves
      we regained some kind of tree-strength that had been severed
the screen lit up with our faces huge hands
reached out to us we lit a tiny fire in the village
that is when my mother María danced an incredible
inappropriate Polka at the center of the plaza (How could that be?
She died decades ago!)
I was expecting parables on the Three Treasures
I was running from the bombs I was delirious for shelter
Outside everything was on fire and the gasman was after me

Imagine that Why me? I said. Why me! But it was no use
so I ran in here
so I crouched under the seats
next to a woman in an emeraldine scaly dress
she was calm & stunning &
strumming a pearl-edged ten-string Stella
you're Ava Gardner I said where's the exit?

This *is* the exit.

poem
by poem

## Poema por poema

— *en memoria de*
*Cynthia Hurd, Susie Jackson, Ethel Lance,*
*Rev. DePayne Middleton-Doctor,*
*Hon. Rev. Clementa Pinckney,*
*Tywanza Sanders, Rev. Daniel Simmons Sr.,*
*Rev. Sharonda Singleton, Myra Thompson*
*muertos a tiros mientras asistían a la iglesia en*
*Charleston, SC (6-18-2015), QEPD*

poema por    poema
podemos acabar con la violencia
todos los días      después
        día tras día

9 abatidos en Charleston, Carolina del Sur
no son 9 siguen
todos
                vivos
no lo sabemos

    tienes un poema que ofrecer
está hecho de acción — debes
buscarlo            salir

corriendo y darle tu vida
cuando lo encuentres      tráelo
de vuelta — sopla sobre él

cárgalo más alto que la ciudad en que vives
cuando la sangre   corra
no preguntes      si

          es tu sangre    está
hecha de
        9          gotas
                   hónralas
lávalas impide
su caída

## Poem by Poem

— *in memory of*
*Cynthia Hurd, Susie Jackson, Ethel Lance,*
*Rev. DePayne Middleton-Doctor,*
*Hon. Rev. Clementa Pinckney,*
*Tywanza Sanders, Rev. Daniel Simmons Sr.,*
*Rev. Sharonda Singleton, Myra Thompson*
*Shot and killed while at church.*
*Charleston, SC (6-18-2015), RIP*

          poem by    poem
we can end the violence
every day         after
      every other day

9 killed in Charleston, South Carolina
they are not 9 they
are each one
              alive
we do not know

      you have a poem to offer
it is made of action — you must
search for it    run

outside and give your life to it
when you find it   walk it
back — blow upon it

carry it taller than the city where you live
when the blood comes down
do not ask      if

       it is your blood  it
is made of
      9        drops
           honor them
wash them stop them
from falling

## Gracias

Gracias to my parents, Lucha and Felipe, relentless in their blessings, kindness, words and love.

Gracias to all my dear ones — my partner, Margarita, children, grandchildren and great-grandchildren.

Gracias to my sisters, Concha and Sarita, nieces, nephews, cousins and aunt Ester, still standing strong.

Gracias to my sisters-in-law and brothers-in-law for opening their doors and setting up the table.

Gracias to my teachers, colleagues, my poetry and art families and all the little cafés that were open.

Gracias to all bookstore families and community centers that work so hard for others in need.

Gracias to all the librarians who were generous since day one.

Gracias to my editor, Elaine Katzenberger, so diligent, so embracing.

Gracias to my book agent, Kendra Marcus, who has encouraged me non-stop.

Gracias to all the schools that I have visited and all the writers' teams and programs across the nation.

Gracias to all community activists for voice-rich children, young peoples and rising communities.

Gracias to all the reporters, interviewers, online bloggers and writers and TV crews.

Gracias to Governor Brown, the California Arts Council, the NEA, the Guggenheim Memorial Foundation, PEN and CPITS, for supporting me through the years.

Also, a big gracias to Tom Lutz at the *LA Review of Books*, Carmen Gimenez-Smith and John Chavez, Christopher Buckley at the *Miramar Journal*, Paco Marquez at the *Washington Square Review*, and Barbara Fischer at the *Boston Review*, Academy of American Poets and the Poetry Foundation for their immense generosity.

To my dear, dear friends — for all of you.

All animals and plants, mountains, open country, oceans and skies — gracias.

You have sustained me.

I want to thank Lauro Flores, whom I have known for many years, with a super-gracias, for translating a number of these poems into Spanish.

And you.

★★

Why dwell in the Blue Mountain
I laugh without answering . . .

— *Li Po, from "Blue Mountain"*

## Acknowledgments

"Half-Mexican"
Published in *Granta: The Magazine of New Writing*, Issue 114,
February 10, 2011.

"Here and There"
Published on the Academy of American Poets website, April 14,
2015: www.poets.org/poetsorg/poem/here-and-there

"song out here"
Published on the Academy of American Poets website: www.poets.
org/poetsorg/poem/song-out-here

"Jackrabbits, Green Onions & Witches Stew"
Published on the Academy of American website, 2014: www.poets.
org/poetsorg/poem/jackrabbits-green-onions-witches-stew

"Saturday Nite at the Buddhist Cinema"
Published by *Los Angeles Review of Books*, 2015.

"Almost Livin' Almost Dyin'"
Published by *The Offing*, an online literary magazine associated
with the *Los Angeles Review of Books*, March 16, 2015: http://
theoffingmag.com/poetry/almost-livin-almost-dyin

"You & I Belong in this Kitchen"
Published on the Academy of American Poets website, 2012: www.
poets.org/poetsorg/poem/you-i-belong-kitchen

"White Dove — Found Outside Don Teriyaki's"
Published by *Boston Review*, April 5, 2015.

In the late 1960s, Juan Felipe Herrera became involved with the new spoken word and street *teatro* Civil Rights movement, reading and performing at schools, prisons, farmworker camps and many college campuses across the nation. In almost every city where he has lived or has visited, Juan Felipe founded spoken word multi-genre performance troupes: Teatro Tolteca in Los Angeles, 1971; TROKA in San Francisco, 1983; Teatro Zapata in Fresno, 1992; Manikrudo in Humbolt, 1996; and the Verbal Coliseum in Riverside, 2007. A number of chronicles from this period of public experiment are included in *187 Reasons Mexicanos Can't Cross the Border: Undocuments 1971–2007* (City Lights Books, 2007). He has also sculpted many language-centered texts, collected in *Exiles of Desire, Akrílica, Border-Crosser with a Lamborghini Dream* and the award-winning *Half of the World in Light: New and Selected Poems*. At the heart of his work is the poet as technician of multiple registers, advocate of multicultural voices and, as Thich Nhat Hanh says, devotee of inter-being, that is, tearing down the walls that separate us personally, culturally and globally.

With twenty-nine books published in poetry, spoken word, novels for young adults and collections for children, Juan Felipe Herrera continues to work for all audiences. His recent awards include the Guggenheim Fellowship, the National Book Critics Circle Award, the Latino International Award, the PEN USA Award and the Josephine Miles Pen/Oakland Award. His recent book, *Portrait of Hispanic American Heroes*, was awarded the Pura Belpré Honors Award. He is a member of the Board of Chancellors of the Academy of American Poetry and recently completed his appointment as the California Poet Laureate. He is a Professor Emeritus of creative writing at UC-Riverside and CSU-Fresno. He lives in Fresno with his partner, poet Margarita Robles.

Son of Mexican farmworkers, born in Fowler, California, Juan Felipe Herrera was invited to serve as the Poet Laureate of the United States in 2015.

"Los Angeles Barrio Sonnet for Wanda Coleman"
Published by the *Los Angeles Review of Books*, November 23, 2013.

"Bisbee Poetry Festival, Southern Arizona, 1985"
Published by the *Los Angeles Review of Books*, January 5, 2013.

"Hey Phil"
Published by the *Los Angeles Review of Books*, February 16, 2015.

"Tomorrow I Leave to El Paso"
Published on the Academy of American Poets website, 2010; edited
by Shelley Taylor and Abraham Smith: www.poets.org/poetsorg/
poem/tomorrow-i-leave-el-paso-texas

"[untitled, unfettered___"
Published by *American Poets, The Journal of the Academy of American
Poets,* Spring-Summer 2014, Vol. 46.

"it can begin with clouds,"
Published in *Angels of the Americlypse: An Anthology of Latin@
Writing.* Edited by Carmen Giménez Smith and John Chávez
(Denver: Counterpath Press, 2014).

"Ourselves"
Published in *Angels of the Americlypse: An Anthology of Latin@
Writing.* Eds. Giménez Smith and Chávez.

"Numbers, Patterns, Movements & Being"
Published in *Miramar.* Editor-in-Chief Christopher Buckley.
Number 3, 2014.

[original title page]

# Lessons in Truth

## by H. Emilie Cady

### *Lee's Summit, Mo., Unity School of Christianity*

### *[1894]*

First published 1894

Republished 2008 by Forgotten Books

*www.forgottenbooks.org*

# DID YOU KNOW...?

*You can read any and all of our <u>thousands</u> of books online for*

# **<u>FREE</u>**

*Just visit:*

### ***www.forgottenbooks.org***